AMPHETAMINES AND ECSTASY

Susan Elliot-Wright

W

HODDER
Wayland

an imprint of Hodder Children's Books

White-Thomson Publishing Ltd,
2-3 St Andrew's Place, Lewes,
East Sussex BN7 1UP

Published in Great Britain in 2004 by Hodder
Wayland, an imprint of Hodder Children's
Books

This book was produced for White-Thomson
Publishing Ltd by Ruth Nason.

Design: Carole Binding
Picture research: Glass Onion Pictures

British Library Cataloguing in Publication Data
Elliot-Wright, Susan
    Amphetamines and Ecstasy. - (Health
    Issues) 1. Amphetamines - Physiological
    effect - Juvenile literature 2. Ecstasy (Drug)
    - Physiological effect - Juvenile literature
    3. Amphetamine abuse - Juvenile literature
    I. Title 613.8'3
ISBN 0 7502 4489 5

Printed by C&C Offset Printing Co., Ltd., China

Hodder Children's Books
A division of Hodder Headline Limited
338 Euston Road, London NW1 3BH

Acknowledgements

The author and publishers thank the following for their permission to reproduce photographs and
illustrations: Corbis: cover, pages 1 and 13 (Lawrence Manning), 4 (Jim Cummins), 8 (Campbell
William/Corbis Sygma), 22 (Dex Images), 28 (Lawrence Manning), 32 (Brooklyn Production), 35
(Yang Liu), 46 (Jonathan Torgovnik), 48 (Rob Lewine), 53 (Chuck Savage), 57 (Dennis Galante), 59
(Tom Stewart); Angela Hampton Family Life Picture Library: page 50; Photofusion: pages 16 (Lisa
Woollett), 55 (Paul Baldesare); Popperfoto.com: pages 11, 34, 38; Rex Features: pages 27 (Sipa
Press), 30 (John Powell); Science Photo Library: pages 7, 14 (BSIP/Jacopin), 17 (Tek Image), 18
(Gusto), 21, 36 (Alain Dex, Publiphoto Diffusion), 41 (Damien Lovegrove), 45 (Larry Mulvehill), 49
(Martin Riedl); Topham/ImageWorks: page 43; Topham Picturepoint: page 25. The illustrations on
pages 9 and 37 are by Carole Binding.

Note: Photographs illustrating the case studies in this book were posed by models.

Every effort has been made to trace copyright holders. However, the publishers apologise for any
unintentional omissions and would be pleased in such cases to add an acknowledgement in any
future editions.

Contents

Introduction
Amphetamine use today

Many drugs, such as cannabis, heroin and cocaine, are frequently in the news, and you will almost certainly have come across some discussion and debate about them. Amphetamines tend not to get as much publicity, and it is possible that you may not even have heard of them before. Yet they are taken by around 250,000 regular users in Britain, and 750,000 in America. There are considerably more 'occasional' users.

Amphetamines are a group of man-made drugs known as stimulants, which means that they stimulate or excite the brain and body, making the person using them feel unnaturally alert, overactive and talkative. Amphetamines tend to speed everything up, which is where they get their most common nickname, 'speed'. Users also report a sense of wellbeing, confidence and even euphoria. These feelings are sometimes described as an 'amphetamine high'. The unpleasant side of this 'high' is the 'low' that inevitably follows. When people 'come down' from amphetamines, they can feel physically and mentally drained, and often report feeling depressed.

Ecstatic

Some experiences in life make us feel extraordinarily happy and triumphant. Some amphetamine users report that the drug makes them feel like that. However, in their case, the feeling is not genuine, and it is followed by a 'crash'. They are also risking long-lasting damage to their health.

st date shown below.

Drug groups

There are three main types of drug that people use for non-medical reasons:

Stimulants   *These act on the central nervous system and increase brain activity. For example: cocaine, crack, amphetamines, nicotine, ecstasy.*

Depressants   *These act on the central nervous system and slow down brain activity. For example: heroin, gases, glues, tranquillizers, alcohol.*

Hallucinogenic   *This type of drug can make people see or hear things that aren't really there. For example: cannabis, LSD, magic mushrooms.*

Amphetamines and the law

Amphetamine is classified as a 'class B' drug in the UK and a 'schedule 2' drug in the USA. This means that the drug:

- has an accepted medical use if prescribed by a doctor;
- is considered to have a high potential for abuse;
- if abused, carries a high risk of physical or psychological dependence.

The maximum sentence for possessing class B drugs in the UK is five years' imprisonment and an unlimited fine. For supplying or trafficking, the maximum sentence is 14 years' imprisonment and an unlimited fine. If amphetamine is prepared for injection, it becomes a class A or schedule 1 drug. This is the group of drugs that are considered to be the most dangerous and for which there are higher penalties.

Ecstasy

The one type of amphetamine you will almost certainly have heard of is MDMA, more commonly known as 'ecstasy'. Although ecstasy is strictly speaking an amphetamine, it is different in several ways from the other drugs we call amphetamines. So, to avoid confusion, we look at ecstasy separately, in Chapter 2.

Medical uses of amphetamines

Amphetamines were originally developed as a
medical treatment for various conditions,
although their effectiveness for most of these
has since been questioned or, in some
cases, disproved. There are still a few
conditions for which amphetamine-
based drugs can be legally
prescribed, although the majority
of amphetamine use is non-medical,
and therefore illegal. We explore the
history of amphetamines and their medical
use in Chapter 3.

*'Everyone was doing
speed. It was going to be
a three-day rave, and I didn't
want to miss any of it. But I felt
like death for about two
weeks afterwards.'
(Natalie, aged 17)*

Amphetamine abuse

People use amphetamines for many different reasons,
from wanting to stay awake all night studying, to wanting
to party for days, to wanting to lose weight. Some people
use them because they think their friends will think them
'chicken' if they do not. Chapter 4 discusses why people
resort to using amphetamines, and also considers other
ways of dealing with the stresses and strains of twenty-
first-century life. There is also some advice for people
who feel that they are being pressured into doing
something they don't really want to do – how to
say 'no'.

One of the big mistakes people make
about amphetamines is to think that,
because they are not as addictive as,
say, heroin, they are safe. It is
true that there are relatively few
deaths from amphetamine overdose,
but people can die as a result of using
amphetamines. There are a number of health
problems associated with amphetamine use,
some quite serious. Some users take amphetamines
intravenously. This means they inject the drug straight
into their veins. People who do this are at risk of various
health problems such as skin infections and collapsed

*'I used to hang out
with these guys who were
real speed-freaks. They just never
stopped, Man. But when they started
shooting the stuff up [injecting the drug
into the veins], that's when I got
scared. I don't want to die,
right?' (Kieran,
aged 18)*

veins. If they share needles, they risk becoming infected with HIV. Chapter 5 looks at how amphetamines can affect someone's health and general wellbeing.

Depending on where you live, you may be aware of drug treatment centres in your area. You may have problems with amphetamine use yourself, or you may know someone who is having difficulty controlling their use. Chapters 6 and 7 look at the nature of addiction and dependence, and at various ways of helping the person break that dependency, possibly with professional help.

Often, when somebody has a problem with drugs or alcohol, they are unable to see that problem clearly for themselves. This may mean that what they say about a certain drug, or a particular aspect of drug use, is less than accurate. The purpose of this book is to provide straightforward information about amphetamines and their effects. Hopefully, it will answer any questions you may have and clear up some of the myths about amphetamine use – like, for example, 'it's not addictive, so it can't hurt you.' It can hurt you, you can become dependent and you can even die from using amphetamines.

Powder

Amphetamines are usually sold in the form of powder. Many users take the drug by snorting, which means sniffing it into their nose.

Help

If you need more information about amphetamines, or if you know someone who might need help, the organizations listed on page 62 may be useful.

1 What are amphetamines?
A lesser-known drug

Amphetamines are a group or 'family' of synthetic (man-made) stimulant drugs. Although all types of amphetamines have similar chemical properties and effects, they vary in the way they are manufactured and in their strength. The main types are amphetamine, dextroamphetamine and methamphetamine.

Some types of amphetamine are or have been available on prescription, to treat illness (more about their medical use in Chapter 3). They have trade names such as Benzedrine, Dexedrine and Methadrine. Amphetamines are also used recreationally: in other words, they are used just to get 'high', rather than for any medical reason. Some street or slang names for amphetamines include speed, whiz, uppers, crank, crystals, amph, meth, base, billy, bennies, sulphate and ice.

Inhaling speed
One of the methods people use to take amphetamines is to heat the drug in a glass tube so that they can inhale the vapour.

Street amphetamine usually comes as an off-white, yellowish or pinkish powder or a putty-like substance known as 'base'. The powders may only be around 20 per cent pure: in other words, only one-fifth of the powder is amphetamine. The rest could be anything from dried baby milk to rat poison. This means that anyone taking the drug is also risking the effects of the additives, any one of which may be a poison in itself. Sometimes, amphetamine is mixed with other stimulants, such as caffeine. This is also dangerous as it increases the stimulant effect, putting a strain on the body's organs.

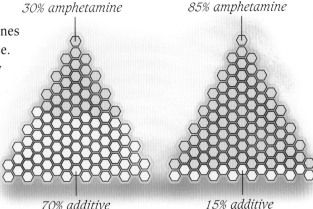

30% amphetamine   *85% amphetamine*

70% additive   *15% additive*

Someone using street amphetamines is also at risk of accidental overdose. Let's say that they always buy from the same person, and the drug is always about the same strength: for example, 30 per cent amphetamine and 70 per cent a relatively harmless additive. Then one day, maybe, they buy the drug from a different person. Let's assume that the additive is still harmless, but this time, what they buy is 85 per cent amphetamine and 15 per cent additive. Suddenly, their body gets nearly three times the amount that it is used to. As you can see, there are lots of dangers.

Different doses

The powders sold as amphetamines are 'bulked out' with differing amounts of additives.

Base tends to be stronger than amphetamine powder, which is often around 50 per cent pure. Methamphetamine, a very strong form of the drug, can be up to 97 per cent pure. It comes as a white powder, crystals (known as 'ice') or tablets.

The powders can be snorted (sniffed up the nose), smoked, inhaled (heated on foil to produce a vapour, which is breathed in) or dissolved and injected intravenously (directly into a vein). Base amphetamine is often swallowed, but apparently tastes disgusting. Because of the nasty bitter taste, it is usually 'bombed' – wrapped in a cigarette paper and then swallowed.

The effects of taking amphetamines

Although you may not know much about amphetamines, you will probably have heard of their most widely-used street name, 'speed'. This nickname describes the effect that amphetamines have on the person who takes them – they speed everything up!

As with any drug, the effects of taking amphetamines vary from person to person. Generally, someone taking amphetamines is likely to experience increased blood pressure, faster breathing and heart rate, and a feeling of boundless energy. They may also become talkative, restless and fidgety. The drug can give a sudden 'rush' of pleasure, a sense of euphoria and a feeling of general wellbeing. The user often feels alert, full of confidence and able to achieve anything.

How quickly and how strongly these effects are felt depends largely on how the drugs are taken. Injecting straight into the bloodstream produces almost instant effects. This is the same if the amphetamine is smoked: the drug enters the bloodstream via the lungs and is carried to the heart, from where it is pumped around the body. It then reaches the brain within seconds, causing an

Methamphetamine and ice

Methamphetamine (meth) is similar in chemical structure and behaviour to amphetamine, but it has a much stronger effect. Meth can easily be converted to crystals, which are called 'ice' because they look a bit like rock salt or ice chips. The crystals are usually smoked or can be injected. The lighted crystals turn to liquid and produce a vapour that can be inhaled, entering the bloodstream via the lungs and rushing the drug to the brain to produce a fast, intense 'high'. This is often followed by a severe crash.

Ice is particularly powerful, as it often has a very high purity. This is due to the difficulty of cutting additives and bulking agents with crystals. Ice is thought to be highly addictive, as the body quickly develops a tolerance. This means that more and more is needed to get the same effects. Long-term use can cause psychological problems, such as paranoia, hallucinations and delusions.

Ice is used in the UK, but (at the moment, at least) is more common in the USA. In Hawaii, addiction to ice is growing fast. It is estimated that 10-15 per cent of Hawaii's population of 1.25 million are users. Dr Andrew Overden of the University of Hawaii believes the problem is in part due to social conditions such as underemployment, inequality in education and difficulties with housing. 'Some people have two or three jobs just to pay their way,' he says. 'It's not hard to see the temptation of ice for them.'

intense 'rush'. The effects from snorting take a few minutes to kick in. This is because the drug enters the bloodstream via the membranes of the nose. Someone who swallows amphetamines will feel the effects after about 15-20 minutes.

Taking amphetamines can cause some really unpleasant effects: for example, dry mouth, increased sweating, headaches, anxiety and insomnia. Some people suffer panic attacks, where they suddenly feel anxious or frightened, they may sweat or shiver, and they start to breathe very quickly (called hyperventilating). Others find that amphetamines make them irritable and hostile. Amphetamines are often associated with violent behaviour (more about this in Chapter 5).

What happens to the brain?

Amphetamines cause certain chemicals to be released within the central nervous system (the brain and spinal cord). For example, the nerve endings release noradrenaline, a chemical that increases the rate and depth of breathing and raises blood pressure by constricting the blood vessels (tightening them by making them narrower).

Melting the ice

In 2003 a large quantity of methamphetamine hydrochloride ('ice'), seized by police in the Philippines, was poured into a drum to be destroyed by burning.

Dopamine is a chemical which is naturally released by the body in response to pleasurable experiences. It acts as a chemical messenger, creating vivid, positive memories of the pleasurable experience, and making the brain keen to repeat it. When amphetamines are taken, more dopamine than usual is released. This makes the brain start to associate amphetamines with pleasure.

This sense of pleasure, together with feelings of energy and alertness, makes amphetamines attractive to some people. Users can stay up all night, working, studying, talking or dancing. They don't need to sleep or eat, can get loads done in a short space of time and may feel cheerful and confident, as if they can conquer the world. It sounds great, you may think. But what goes up, as they say, must come down. And when you come down from an amphetamine high, you can really crash.

Pay-back time

You may remember from your physics lessons that 'energy cannot be created or destroyed'; it may help to remember this when you are trying to understand how amphetamines affect people. All that 'extra' energy that amphetamines seem to give isn't really extra at all – it's merely 'borrowed' from the body's natural energy stores. This means that when the effects wear off, the body needs to recover all the energy that has been squandered by the effects of the drug. And so coming down from an amphetamine high leaves the user feeling drained, or wiped out.

As the effects wear off, the person may feel lethargic to the point of exhaustion, depressed and tense. They may also experience mood swings and paranoia. Often, people are tempted to repeat the dose more often in order to avoid these symptoms. This can lead to dependence on the drug.

How widespread is amphetamine use?

Amphetamine use, both medical and recreational, was fairly common in the 1950s and early 1960s, in both Britain and the USA. In Britain, the suit-and-tie-wearing,

scooter-riding 'Mods' regularly took amphetamines so that they could stay awake to take advantage of the new all-night clubs that were appearing in the major cities. In the USA, it was the 'Beats' who took amphetamines. The Beats were a group of writers and artists who felt that post-war America was dull and boring. They took amphetamines in the hope of feeling some excitement and inspiration. As other street drugs, such as marijuana and LSD, became popular in the late 1960s, amphetamine use declined. It increased again in the 1980s as the dance culture began to grow. Clubbers wanted to stay awake all night, and there was concern about the purity and safety of some street ecstasy, so amphetamines seemed a better option.

Today, although amphetamine use is not as widespread as it once was, recreational use has again become fairly popular. We will look more closely at the possible reasons for this in Chapter 4, including low cost, the relatively small risk of overdose, and the drugs' availability. Amphetamines are easily made in illegal laboratories in the country where they are sold.

All through the night

Amphetamine use increased as night clubs where people could stay dancing into the early hours of the morning became fashionable.

2 Ecstasy (MDMA)
A close relation

Ecstasy is one of the more common names for methylenedioxymethamphetamine (MDMA). It is also known as XTC, Adam, doves and E. Strictly speaking, it is a member of the amphetamine 'family', and is similar in chemical structure to methamphetamine. However, ecstasy has both stimulant and hallucinogenic properties, whereas amphetamine is purely a stimulant.

MDMA stimulates the release of serotonin, a 'feel-good' chemical that occurs naturally in the brain. Serotonin is involved in various brain functions to do with mood and emotion. Scientists now believe that MDMA damages the parts of the nerves that transmit serotonin. This could be why some people who take it end up suffering from depression and anxiety.

History

MDMA was first synthesized (artificially created) in 1914 by a German drug company. It was originally intended to be an appetite suppressant, although it was never actually marketed. Nothing more was done with the drug until the early 1950s, when it underwent testing by the US military. The rumour was that they were considering using it as a 'truth drug'. The idea was that the drug could be given to enemy prisoners so that when they were questioned, they would talk openly about their side's weapons, plans and so on.

Nerve to nerve

Chemical messengers like serotonin cross from one nerve cell in your brain to another. This diagram shows how an electrical signal in the nerve cell at the top causes serotonin in the cell to be released. It is captured by receptors (yellow) on the next nerve cell. Later it is reabsorbed into the first nerve cell.

It was then tried on a small scale by some American therapists. They too felt that it helped people to relax and 'open up', therefore encouraging patients to talk about their problems. Some therapists in Switzerland still use the drug in this way. In the UK and USA, however, there is currently no recognized medical use for MDMA.

By the late 1970s, MDMA had made its way to the street as a recreational drug. Its dangers soon became apparent and it was classified as 'class A' in the UK and 'schedule 1' in the USA. Penalties for possession or dealing are high. The drug is produced illegally on a large scale, often in the country in which it is sold, although large amounts are smuggled into the USA from Western Europe.

What does it look like?

MDMA comes mainly as tablets or capsules. The appearance varies, ranging from brown, pink or white tablets, to clear, red and yellow or red and black capsules. There is often a brand name or logo, such as butterflies, lightning bolts and four-leaf clovers. It may also be sold as a powder. The drug is usually swallowed, although the powder may occasionally be smoked or snorted. Injecting MDMA is very rare.

How many people use ecstasy?

In 2002, the European Monitoring Centre for Drugs and Drug Addiction estimated that around 3,500,000 adults in the European Union had used ecstasy. In the UK specifically, between 500,000 and 1,000,000 teenagers claim to have tried it at least once. The UK government estimates that over 1,000,000 ecstasy tablets are taken every weekend.

In the USA, the National Household Survey on Drug Abuse found that 6,400,000 people over the age of 12 reported having used ecstasy at some point, with 2,500,000 teenagers claiming to have tried it at least once.

Short-term effects

Like amphetamines, MDMA raises blood pressure, increases the heart rate and breathing and can keep people awake all night. Unlike amphetamines, it also causes people to feel deeply relaxed. They may feel warmly towards other people, and also have a strong sense of empathy – when you feel you understand the other person very well. Like amphetamines, MDMA also makes people feel they do not need to eat or sleep, and this makes it a popular 'party' or 'club' drug. The effects can last for hours. Users often say they feel a 'rush' of wellbeing, followed by a sense of calm. Sometimes, they feel that they can hear more clearly and see colours much more vividly. Other effects include dilated pupils, teeth clenching, nausea, sweating, dry mouth and overheating.

'The first time I used E was fantastic. I had a really great time. But the next day I couldn't sleep and weird stuff started going on in my head. I was seeing strange creatures, like I was possessed by some demon.' (Clare, aged 16)

Club drug

Nightclubs are an environment where people may be offered ecstasy.

Long-term effects

Compared with other drugs, we do not know much about the long-term effects of ecstasy use. To a certain extent, those using it are human guinea pigs. Users often argue that ecstasy is safe, but there is increasing evidence to suggest that this is far from true. Unpleasant side effects may be experienced immediately, or may kick in as the drug wears off. These may include nausea, chills, sweating, muscle cramps, teeth clenching, blurred vision and hallucinations. Ecstasy has also been linked to liver and kidney problems.

Some of the side effects can last for weeks after the drug was taken, and may be similar to those experienced by amphetamine users. They include anxiety, sleeplessness, depression, confusion and paranoia.

There is still a lot of research into the effects of MDMA. Some recent studies suggest that heavy use may cause memory problems, depression and problems with learning. There is no way of telling whether these effects are permanent, but research suggests that they are certainly long-lasting. Recent studies also suggest that MDMA may cause long-term brain damage. Monkeys who were given the drug twice a day for four days showed signs of brain damage which was still evident six to seven years later.

Unknown effects
Current research suggests that the long-term effects of using ecstasy may be long-lasting and severe.

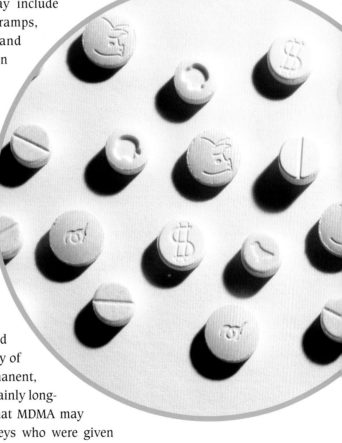

Danger of dehydration and death

One of the main dangers of ecstasy use is the risk of severe dehydration. This is where the body loses fluid more quickly than it is being replaced. Our bodies are made up of almost two-thirds water, so you can see how important it is for us to stay 'hydrated' (keep our fluid levels up).

Liquid level
Drinking enough water is one of the most important parts of keeping your body in good health.

Water is lost from the body through natural processes, such as when you sweat or urinate. Sometimes more water than usual is lost. This may happen because the person is ill, such as when they lose water due to vomiting or diarrhoea. Or it may be due to other factors, such as overheating. Normal body temperature is around 36.6°C. When the body gets hotter than this, it cools itself by sweating, and by widening the capillaries (tiny blood vessels) in the skin. This causes the blood to cool faster. The trouble is that MDMA affects this cooling system by causing the blood vessels to narrow, thereby reducing heat loss instead of increasing it.

Taking ecstasy raises the body temperature and can cause sudden and excessive sweating; dancing energetically raises the temperature further and causes more sweating. So, when someone takes ecstasy, they will already be in danger of overheating. They then dance, often for long periods without a break, and lose a lot of fluid through sweating. If they don't keep their fluids topped up, they can become seriously dehydrated. If you were to drive a car for thousands of miles on a hot day without topping up the water levels, the engine would overheat and possibly seize up altogether. When a human body reaches 40°C, the body will sweat profusely. If that fluid is not replaced, the person is at risk of heat stroke. This can lead to coma, and death due to kidney failure, heart failure or heat-related damage to the brain.

When ecstasy is something else

There is also a risk of swallowing something that is not, in fact, MDMA. Some ecstasy tablets have been found to contain a mixture of MDMA and amphetamine or another stimulant drug. Some tablets have even been found to be dog-worming tablets or fish-tank cleaners!

Who uses MDMA?

Ecstasy is known as a 'club drug' and is particularly popular with those who want to dance all night. Users also claim that it lowers inhibitions, making them feel more relaxed and cheerful, yet still energetic. This is why it is widely seen as a 'young person's drug', with most users in the 16-24 age group. Also, it is fairly cheap – between £4 and £10 per pill in the UK, depending on the area. The cost in the USA is around $20 a tablet.

Staying safe

There have been a number of dance safety campaigns following deaths from taking MDMA. Many clubs now have 'chill-out' rooms where dancers can relax and recover. Dancers who have taken ecstasy are advised to sip a pint of water per hour, to replace fluid lost by sweating. It can be dangerous to drink too much too quickly.

Deaths

There have been around 90 deaths from ecstasy in the UK, often due to organ failure as a result of heat stroke after dancing. Other causes of deaths from ecstasy include heart failure due to increased heart rate and blood pressure, internal bleeding, and respiratory collapse and/or organ failure as a result of the effects of MDMA on blood clotting.

3 The history of amphetamines
From medicine to menace

An early form of amphetamine was created in Germany in 1887. It was called phenylisopropylamine. However, it was not developed and used as a medicine until 40 years later. Scientists had been looking for a new drug to treat asthma for some time. During the late nineteenth and early twentieth centuries, asthma was treated with adrenaline, also called epinephrine. This drug stimulates the body's 'fight or flight' response, which triggers dilation (widening) of the airways in the lungs. This makes breathing easier, and so the treatment was useful for the breathing difficulties experienced by people with asthma. The problem was that the drug could only be given by injection as, when taken by mouth, it was destroyed in the stomach and intestine before it could be absorbed by the body.

In the 1920s, Ko Kuei Chen and Carl Schmidt, two chemists working for Eli Lilly and Co., began to investigate the ma huang plant, which had been used for many years in Chinese herbal medicine to treat wheezing. They

The 'fight or flight' response

This is an ancient response that we have inherited from our 'hunter-gatherer' ancestors. It is the body's way of preparing us for danger. In times of fear and distress, the body releases the hormone adrenaline, which triggers the 'fight or flight' response.

Adrenaline speeds up the heart, so that it pumps more blood to the muscles in the arms and legs to give them greater strength. Adrenaline also causes the airways in the lungs to dilate (widen), so that breathing may be faster and deeper. This enables the person to move more quickly. The idea is that, faced with a sabre-toothed tiger or an axe-wielding maniac, the body reacts by becoming ready to 'fight' or to take 'flight', running fast enough to escape.

isolated the plant's active ingredient and called it 'ephedrine', as its effects were similar to those of epinephrine. Unlike epinephrine, ephedrine could be given by mouth, and so it quickly became a popular treatment for asthma. Ephedrine was successful, but the ma huang plant was becoming rare, and so scientists began to look for an alternative.

An asthma cure with a difference

In 1927, a research chemist called Gordon Alles was looking for ways to synthesize ephedrine when he discovered a compound that worked in a similar way. The compound was called Alpha-Methyl-PHenyl-EThylAMINE – and Alles shortened it, as the capital letters show, to amphetamine. He found that amphetamine raised blood pressure, increased the heart rate and caused widening of the airways. He also noticed that it made people less tired, increased alertness and gave a sense of euphoria. What was more, it could be taken by mouth or inhaled straight into the lungs.

In 1932, amphetamine was marketed as Benzedrine, an over-the-counter (non-prescription) treatment for asthma, hay fever and even colds. The treatment came in the form of an inhaler. This was a device that could be held up to the face so that the Benzedrine vapours could be inhaled.

Benzedrine quickly become popular as its side effects – alertness and euphoria – became more widely known. Some people began using it recreationally, rather than as a medicine. This was done by opening up the inhaler and sniffing the amphetamine-soaked paper strip inside. People who wanted a more intense effect – known as an 'amphetamine rush' – would chew on or swallow the strip.

Short of breath

An asthma attack occurs when the airways in the lungs become narrow and inflamed. Asthma is a common illness, which can be painful and debilitating, and so scientists were keen to find a treatment.

Using the inhaler's contents became particularly popular among college students. As well as using it to get high, they also found it had another purpose. They found that, by using Benzedrine, they were able to stay awake all night studying. They also felt it helped them to concentrate, so it became very popular at exam time.

Night study
Students may try to keep themselves awake until very late, to continue revising for exams.

A wonder drug

By the late 1930s, amphetamines were available in tablet form. Amphetamine-based products were being used to treat a variety of conditions, including depression, fatigue and obesity. Amphetamine was particularly effective in treating narcolepsy (where the person suddenly falls asleep at various times during the day). The treatment relied on the fact that amphetamine-based drugs would keep the person alert and awake during the day. The idea was that they would then be so tired at night that they would sleep for long enough to stop them nodding off during the next day. Narcolepsy is quite rare, but is still sometimes treated with an amphetamine called Dexedrine.

In 1937, an American doctor, Charles Bradley, wrote an article for the *American Journal of Psychiatry* about the effects of amphetamine on children with behaviour and attention problems – now known as Attention Deficit Hyperactivity Disorder (ADHD). He noticed that the drug Benzedrine seemed to improve these children's behaviour and their achievement at school. More research was carried out and, in a number of studies, the amphetamine-based drug Ritalin was found to be effective in treating the disorder. Ritalin became available in 1957.

How does Ritalin work?

How, you may wonder, can a drug based on amphetamine – which is a stimulant – help a disorder like hyperactivity, where the child needs to be calmed down rather than stimulated? Doctors are not sure exactly how Ritalin works, but it may be that it corrects a chemical imbalance in the brain. In ADHD, some of the neurones – nerve cells that send chemical 'messages' controlling everything we think, feel and do – work too hard, while others don't work hard enough. So, in someone with ADHD, the part of the brain that tells them when to pay attention to certain activities and ignore others is 'lazy'. Ritalin stimulates the under-worked neurones, so that the child can focus their interest on what is going on around them. This makes them less likely to become bored, restless and fidgety.

The extent of Ritalin use ...

Today, Ritalin is widely used to treat ADHD – some people say too widely. The amount prescribed in the UK increased from 3,000 prescriptions in 1993 to 220,000 in 2002. In the USA, around 4,000,000 children are estimated to be on the drug. The USA is responsible for almost 90 per cent of the Ritalin used worldwide. Some people are worried that giving children psychotropic drugs (drugs that act on the mind and moods, such as stimulants, sedatives and anti-depressants) may actually cause brain damage over time. Others are worried about harmful side effects.

ADHD, like many behavioural disorders, is difficult to diagnose – you can't test for it, and the symptoms are not the same in each child. It's thought that some doctors are under pressure from parents and teachers who are exhausted from coping with difficult and disruptive behaviour. This has led to suggestions that the doctors prescribe the drugs too easily, just to get kids to settle down and get on with their school work.

...and misuse

So far, there has been very little research on the growing problem of Ritalin misuse. However, it is said to be widespread in the USA, with the problem increasing in the UK at an alarming rate. Ritalin pills are crushed and then the powder is either snorted or smoked, or dissolved in water and then heated for injection.

In 2003, a British newspaper reported on children selling Ritalin tablets in the school playground for as little as 50 pence each. In some cases, the report said, the drugs were sold by children who had bullied others into handing over their medication. In other cases, older brothers or sisters had stolen Ritalin prescribed for their younger siblings and were selling it to other children. The paper claimed that British schoolchildren as young as six were becoming hooked on the stimulant drug sold illegally by child dealers.

Pills to perk you up and slim you down

Many amphetamine-based preparations could be bought over the counter and this led to widespread 'self-prescribing', particularly for depression and to help with weight loss. Tired, bored housewives of the 1950s and '60s found that they felt more cheerful and energetic after taking the tablets, which soon became known as 'pep' pills. 'Pep' was a slang term for energy or feeling energized. When people talked of something that made a person feel more lively, they would say that it would 'pep you up'.

Amphetamines were also well known as a slimming aid. They suppressed the appetite and

Cure-all

In 1946, amphetamines were the number-one prescribed medicine in the UK for 39 different ailments, including seasickness, migraine, impotence and fatigue.

It seemed like a wonder drug

'I certainly prescribed amphetamines for my patients in the 1940s and 1950s, and I know my colleagues did, too. There were a number of amphetamine-based drugs which we could give for depression, fatigue and "nerve problems" – what we call "stress" these days. Patients would come in and say that they needed a "tonic" or a "pick-me-up" and these drugs seemed to do the trick at first. Later, we became aware of the side effects – headaches, sleeplessness, mood swings, irritability and depression – the very thing the drugs were supposed to treat! They offered temporary relief, but then the symptoms would return with a few more besides. Many young wives wanted the drugs for slimming. They worked, but the weight loss was only temporary, and the women would usually end up heavier than before. The worst thing was that so many patients became dependent. Amphetamines ruined a lot of lives in those days.'
(Charles, retired family doctor)

apparently increased energy and therefore activity. Therefore, taking them could result in a fairly fast (though temporary) weight loss.

The side effects of long-term amphetamine use – mood swings, extreme fatigue, depression – led to many women becoming dependent on the drugs. They relied on further doses to relieve those unpleasant symptoms, which were in fact being created by amphetamines in the first place.

Amphetamine became a prescription-only drug in 1956 in the UK and in 1965 in the USA. This meant that it became illegal to possess the drug if it had not been prescribed by a doctor. In Sweden, widespread non-medical use of amphetamines led to them being made prescription-only as early as 1939.

Even when you could only get amphetamines if your doctor gave you a prescription, they were seen as a quick fix for weight problems. Doctors were under pressure to supply prescriptions to people (mainly women) who were not particularly overweight. Until quite recently, amphetamine-based drugs were still used in the USA to treat obesity.

Amphetamines and war

Amphetamines were widely used in the Second World War to keep soldiers and pilots awake and alert during long periods of combat. They also relieved the war-weariness sometimes known as 'battle fatigue'. After taking amphetamines, fighting men could walk for longer, run faster and, as the drug suppressed the appetite, could continue for longer without food. Adolf Hitler, the German dictator and Nazi leader, is said to have been on daily amphetamine injections during the war.

Addiction became a huge problem among US, British, German and Japanese soldiers and pilots. In Japan, immediately after the Second World War, supplies of methamphetamine that had been stored for military use became available to the public. This led to the practice of injecting methamphetamine

Healthy ways to control your weight

The safest, healthiest way to control your weight is to eat a sensible, varied diet and take regular daily exercise, such as walking or cycling.

Most of your daily food intake should come from carbohydrates – e.g. rice, pasta, cereals and bread – as they provide most of the energy your body needs to get you through the day. You should also try to eat lots of fresh fruit and vegetables. These are a good source of vitamins and minerals, which help to protect your body against illness. You should eat a couple of portions of protein, such as meat, fish or nuts, for healthy growth and repair, and a similar amount of dairy produce, such as cheese or milk – these are good sources of calcium for healthy bones. Try to keep sugar-based foods, such as sweets, biscuits and cakes, to a minimum. They are fine for an occasional treat, but they do not have any nutritional value and often end up being stored by the body as surplus fat.

Many people who think they are overweight are in fact a perfectly healthy size. If you really are overweight, it's best to cut down on high-fat and sugary foods, and increase the amount of exercise you take, to help burn up any excess fat stored in your body.

becoming more common among the general population, as well as among the many servicemen who had become addicted. In Japan just after the war, 5 per cent of the population aged 15-25 were dependent on the drug.

US soldiers were also given amphetamines during the Korean War (1950-3) and the Vietnam War (1954-76). The US air force continued to prescribe amphetamine tablets – known as 'go-pills' – to combat pilots, in what the military described as 'small, controlled doses', until 1993. This was stopped after reports of crews becoming addicted during the Gulf War (1990-91). In recent years, however, the drug has been reintroduced. The military argue that it is a useful 'medical tool' for pilots in combat.

'It was a shocking state of affairs. Servicemen on all sides had been issued these drugs to keep them awake, and a great many became addicted as a result.'
(Margaret, Second World War historian)

Bad morning, Vietnam
US soldiers serving in Vietnam were given amphetamines to keep up their energy levels.

Even when amphetamines were no longer being prescribed in these ways, the drugs were still popular with young people who used them recreationally – from the scooter-riding 'Mods' of the 1960s to the 'punks' of the 1970s and '80s. Amphetamines are still used as a recreational drug today, particularly among clubbers.

4 Why people use amphetamines
Life in the fast lane

What's the attraction?

As we have seen, the medical use of amphetamines today is restricted to the treatment of a small number of conditions, including narcolepsy and Attention Deficit Hyperactivity Disorder (ADHD). By far the more common use of amphetamines in the twenty-first century is as a recreational or performance-enhancing drug. Amphetamines have been used in these ways for almost as long as they have been around for medical purposes.

Many young people start taking amphetamines because they hear about the apparent confidence boost and extra energy the drugs can provide. They also hear that amphetamines could help them to stay awake – and dancing – all night. For teenagers who are just beginning to explore the adult world of all-night parties, clubs and dance events, the idea of such a boost in pill form can seem very attractive.

What they don't hear about is the 'down' that inevitably follows the amphetamine high. The extra energy isn't really extra – in fact, it is 'borrowed' from the body's energy reserves, and as soon as the effects of the drug wear off, the user starts to feel tired, lethargic and possibly depressed. In long-term users, the side effects can be much

Dance until you drop
There's no harm in staying up late sometimes, if you keep yourself healthy.

Healthy ways to boost your energy

If you are fit and healthy, there's no reason why you should not be able to stay up late and dance all night (well, most of it) once in a while. Keep yourself in peak condition with a little attention to your diet and lifestyle.

- **Sleep**. *Make sure you get enough. The amount each person needs varies, but for adults it's usually eight or nine hours per night. Growing teenagers need more.*

- **Exercise**. *Regular exercise, preferably daily, such as swimming, cycling and walking, will help energize you and keep your heart and lungs working efficiently. If you are not used to exercise, start gently, as it may make you feel tired at first, but you will soon feel the benefits.*

- **Food**. *Eat more fresh fruit and vegetables, especially those that you can eat raw, for example in salads. Many people say that lots of raw food gives a feeling of vitality. Wholegrain bread, rice and pasta are good for long-lasting energy.*

- **Water**. *Drink six to eight glasses a day. Our bodies are made up of almost two-thirds water. Water has many functions in the body, from regulating body temperature to protecting and cushioning the organs and joints. If we don't have enough water in our bodies we become dehydrated and this can make us feel weary. Most of us are dehydrated for most of the time, because we don't drink enough water to replace what is lost normally each day, such as when we sweat or when we pass urine. Cut down on fizzy drinks and anything with caffeine in – the boost you get from caffeine, which is also a stimulant, is temporary, and you are likely to feel worse when it wears off. Caffeine is a 'diuretic', which means that it causes more urine to be produced, also contributing to dehydration.*

more serious, including irritability, anxiety, paranoia and psychological disturbances.

Girls are often attracted by the idea that amphetamines will help them lose weight, and this may work initially, but once the effects of the drugs wear off, the appetite returns and the person goes back to their usual level of activity.

In fact, the person may even be less active than before, especially if they are feeling tired and run down, as often happens after amphetamine use. Amphetamine abuse is not uncommon among fashion models, male as well as female, who take the drugs before a 'photo shoot' so that they will achieve the false, super-thin look that so many magazines desire. Many people in the fashion industry become addicted to amphetamines as a result.

Other reasons why amphetamines are still fairly popular are their cost and availability. At roughly £10-£12 per gram in the UK, and around $30 per gram in the USA, amphetamines are considerably cheaper than other stimulant drugs such as cocaine. Also, because they are usually made in the country in which they are used, they are much easier to get hold of than cocaine, which is smuggled in from other countries. For this reason, some cocaine users turn to amphetamines as a cheaper, easily accessible substitute.

Playground deals
You may be aware of amphetamines, such as Ritalin, changing hands in the school playground. It's important to think about what you would do if you saw this happening.

Peer pressure

Even if a little warning voice in your head is telling you to 'beware', it can be quite hard to be the odd one out if all your friends are taking amphetamines and egging you on to do the same. This is called 'peer pressure', and many adults now say that this was the main reason why they first did something that they really didn't want to do, such as smoking, stealing, taking drugs or having sex before they were ready.

'I got offered these pills at school last term, and I'm like, no way, Man – that stuff can mess with your head.'
(Curtis, aged 16)

You may be offered amphetamines when you are out with your friends; you may be offered amphetamines by your friends. You may even be offered them while you are at school. One of the most common drugs on offer in the school playground at the moment is Ritalin, which is used legitimately to treat ADHD, but which is now frequently abused by young people with easy access to it.

How to say 'No'

Pressure from your peers – your friends, classmates, people you hang out with – can be difficult to resist. Sometimes it's not that they actually say you should be doing something; it's just that they make you feel you are weird if you don't.

If this happens, it's probably best to leave the situation if you can. Alternatively, relax, try to enjoy yourself despite the way you are feeling, and when someone does eventually suggest that you try amphetamines (or cigarettes, or shoplifting or whatever it is that they are doing), don't make excuses like, 'I can't because I've got to get home,' or 'I can't today but maybe next time.' If you do this, they will just keep on at you. Say firmly, 'Thanks, but it's really not my thing.' They might laugh at first or try to intimidate you, but if you stick to your guns, they will soon realize that you are stronger-willed than they are. You may even make them feel rather foolish.

Not recreational, but not medical either

Some people use amphetamines because they think that the drug will enable them to study harder. If they stay awake all night, they think, then surely they will absorb more information and perform better in their exams.

Similarly, shift workers sometimes use amphetamines in order to work more efficiently during the night, when they might normally feel sleepy. There are certain types of job in which amphetamine use is more common. The need to stay awake often leads long-distance lorry drivers to take the drug, and the need to work quickly and intensely for long periods means there is heavy use of amphetamines in the catering industry. Drug users tend to resort to amphetamines when other people might have a cup of coffee.

Staying awake

Hotel and restaurant chefs, kitchen staff and waiters are some examples of workers who need to stay awake, alert and full of energy at times when it is more usual to relax and feel sleepy.

I've been really stupid

'I should be at Uni by now, but I'm re-sitting my A levels instead. I've always loved the sciences, and I want to study marine biology. I'm fascinated by underwater life, and the course is fantastic. You get taken on field trips and they even teach you to dive. I was offered a place at my first choice university and I was feeling great. I was a bit stressed at exam time – everyone was. Then this guy in my year said he'd got some pills – "uppers", he called them. He said they'd give me "an edge", because I'd be able to stay awake for ages and get loads of revision done.

Well, I can't remember how many I took, but I was buzzing for two nights, and then on the third, I went to bed but couldn't sleep. The next day I was wiped out – like I had flu or something. I did the exam, but it was rubbish. I missed the next exam – I just couldn't get out of bed. And the last one, well. I don't even want to talk about it. So here I am, back at school, when I should be having the time of my life at Uni. I can't believe I was so stupid.'
(Dee, aged 18)

Study tips

If you have exams coming up and you need to spend a lot of time studying, here are a few tips to help you.

- *Eat little and often – big meals will make you sluggish. Opt for a snack every three hours or so, to keep your energy up.*

- *Avoid sugary snacks – the energy boost they give is temporary, and you'll feel extra-tired as it wears off.*

- *Take regular exercise – even a ten-minute walk, twice a day, will help.*

- *Take a five-minute 'study break' every hour. Sitting hunched over your books or computer for long periods will give you backache and eyestrain, as well as making you feel tired.*

- *Make sure you get enough sleep – if you're tired, you cannot function efficiently.*

- *Some people find that certain smells act as natural stimulants. Try using a few drops of rosemary or basil oil in an oil burner in the room where you are working – check with your parents first, though.*

Performance enhancing

Amphetamines have also been widely used among sportspeople. They cause an increase in the heart rate, which means that blood is pumped around the body more quickly, providing a temporary increase in energy and stamina. These days, regular drug testing is carried out at sports events to avoid the problem of 'doping' (taking drugs to enhance performance) and many hopefuls are disqualified after failing the tests. In the past, various drugs have resulted in or contributed to the deaths of some sportspeople.

Spoiled sports

At the 1960 Rome Olympics, German cyclist Kurt Jensen collapsed due to heat stroke and subsequently died. An autopsy revealed that he had taken amphetamines shortly beforehand.

British cyclist Tommy Simpson took amphetamines to aid his performance in the 1967 Tour de France. Reports suggest that his death during the race, which was watched by a horrified television audience, was due to heart failure resulting from a combination of amphetamine use and the intense heat of the day.

Testing for drugs

Increasingly, sports organizations check urine samples from athletes, to check that they have not tried to cheat by taking drugs to improve their performance.

Twenty-four seven

In the twenty-first century, we are all under pressure to work, study and play harder than ever before. We are used to round-the-clock television, all-night clubs and bars, and supermarkets that are open all night. Clubbers talk of going out on Friday night and not returning home until Sunday. There are frequent newspaper reports of people 'burning out' in the workplace because they are working 50-hour weeks with no holidays. Even primary schoolchildren are suffering from stress because they feel they are being pressured to perform well in tests.

The trouble is that, if someone wants to slow down, they may feel that the world is moving so quickly that it will move on without them and that they will somehow be left behind. It is perhaps this non-stop culture – the 'twenty-four seven' way of life – that contributes to the popularity of stimulant drugs like amphetamines. People are so worried about not being able to maintain the same levels of work or partying as their colleagues and friends that, instead of naturally slowing down and taking a break when they need it, they take amphetamines to help them keep up.

City life

Modern life, especially in towns and cities, is non-stop and 'open all hours'. This makes it difficult for people to find relaxation.

5 Damage to the body
Speed really can kill

Amphetamines take effect once they enter the brain. Like other stimulants, they affect a part of the central nervous system, called the sympathetic nervous system. The sympathetic nervous system controls many involuntary activities of the glands, organs and other parts of the body. It is responsible for the 'fight or flight' response (see page 20) – the physical changes, such as increased heart rate, blood pressure and breathing, that make us more alert, aware and prepared for action.

The drugs are carried to the brain in the user's blood. Amphetamine is highly soluble in lipids, the fatty acids in the blood. This means that it dissolves quickly in the bloodstream, which distributes it around the body's organs. Because amphetamine is dissolved so quickly, it crosses the 'blood-brain barrier' easily.

Amphetamine that is smoked or inhaled enters the bloodstream via the lungs. The lungs contain thousands of tiny air sacs called alveoli, which are surrounded by

Nasal membranes
When someone snorts amphetamine powder, the drug gets into their bloodstream via the membranes of the nose.

The blood-brain barrier

Tiny blood vessels called capillaries carry blood (and therefore oxygen) to the brain. These capillaries are lined with a tightly packed layer of cells which prevent many substances from crossing into the brain and causing damage. As amphetamine is lipid-soluble (in other words, it dissolves in the blood's fatty acids), it is able to cross through this barrier and enter the brain.

capillaries (tiny blood vessels). The walls of the alveoli are thin, so that oxygen from breathed-in air can pass through into the capillaries, and into the bloodstream. When someone smokes or inhales amphetamine, it passes into the bloodstream with the oxygen, reaching the brain almost immediately.

Amphetamine that is injected straight into the bloodstream also reaches the brain almost immediately. By contrast, amphetamines that are swallowed are absorbed through the intestine before being broken down and passing into the bloodstream. This process takes around 20 minutes, or longer if there is food in the stomach. Therefore, the drug does not reach the brain, and the person does not feel its effects until after 20 minutes or so.

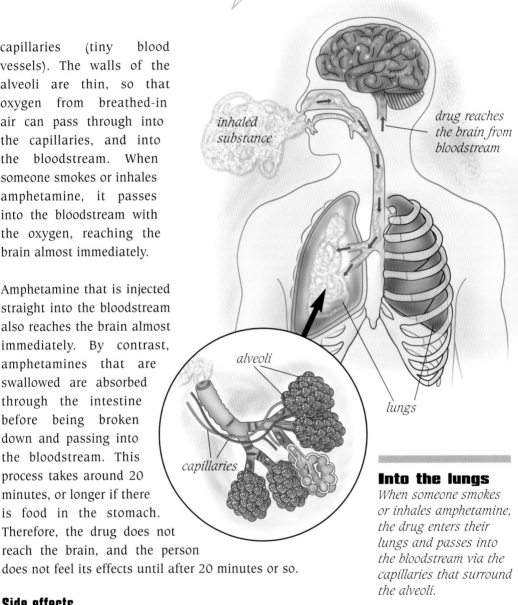

inhaled substance

drug reaches the brain from bloodstream

alveoli

lungs

capillaries

Into the lungs

When someone smokes or inhales amphetamine, the drug enters their lungs and passes into the bloodstream via the capillaries that surround the alveoli.

Side effects

People take amphetamines in order to feel more confident, alert and energetic, as well as for the sense of wellbeing. However, large doses or regular use can cause a number of unpleasant side effects, including addiction and dependence. Addiction is where the body becomes so used to functioning with the drug present that it cannot function properly without it. Dependence is where taking the drug becomes so much a part of someone's life that they feel they cannot stop, even though it is harming them.

When somebody is taking amphetamines regularly, they will sleep less, eat less and use more energy than normal. This can lead to the user becoming tired, anxious and possibly constipated, since the body's systems slow down and become less able to carry out normal functions. Lack of food can lead to malnourishment and also affects the immune system (the body's system of fighting and protecting against infection). This makes amphetamine users more likely to succumb to illness. Lack of sleep also affects the immune system.

Staying safe

Amy's story (below) shows how drugs can spoil a night out with friends. You may never take amphetamines, but you may go to places where other people are taking them. You should know what to do if someone has a bad reaction to them.

I was really scared

'We were going to this new club to celebrate the end of our exams. My friend Leanne had some whiz, and she said we'd have a really great night if we were totally off our heads. I was a bit nervous, but everyone else was up for it, so we all took some. When it kicked in, it felt great – like we could do whatever we wanted, dance all night, sing, whatever. Leanne's brother, Ollie, kept shouting, "I'm the king of the world"– like in the film, Titanic. Anyway, we were having a great time, then Ollie started getting shaky and twitchy, and saying mad stuff like "I know what you're up to" and "I know you've told the police". Then he started breathing really fast and loud, so we took him outside. I thought he was going to die. Someone dialled 999 and the paramedics came and put him in the ambulance. They took him to the hospital and, of course, someone phoned Leanne and Ollie's mum, so before long, all our parents knew, and we all got grounded. Fortunately, Ollie was OK, but the whole thing just wasn't worth it.'
(Amy, aged 16)

Larger doses or particularly strong forms of amphetamine, such as methamphetamine, can result in headaches, sweating, dizziness, irregular breathing, mental confusion and loss of co-ordination. Large doses may also cause a stroke. This is where a blood vessel in the brain bursts, due to the increased blood pressure caused by the drug. A stroke can leave a person disabled, or the person may die.

What to do if someone has a bad reaction after taking amphetamines

If they feel tense and panicky:

- *Calm them and reassure them that the feelings will pass.*
- *Try to steer them away from crowds, noisy music and bright lights.*
- *If they start breathing very quickly, calm them down and encourage them to take long, slow breaths.*

Speed and ecstasy affect the body's temperature control. If someone using these drugs dances energetically without taking breaks or drinking enough fluids, their body could overheat and dehydrate (lose too much body fluid). Warning signs include: cramps, fainting, headache or sudden tiredness. If this happens:

- *Move the person to a cooler area, perhaps outside.*
- *Remove excess clothing and try to cool them down by wiping them with a cloth soaked in cool water.*
- *Get them to sip (not gulp) about a pint of non-alcoholic fluid an hour – water's fine, but try to include some fruit juice or sports drinks, which will help replace the minerals lost through sweating.*
- *If they lose consciousness, or if you are worried, call an ambulance and explain what has happened. Don't worry about the legal side of things – you won't get in trouble and may save a life. Ambulance staff and paramedics will be more interested in treating the patient than telling the police that someone has been using drugs.*

Amphetamines and mental health

Regular, heavy use of amphetamines can lead to mental health problems such as depression and mood swings. These can continue even after use of the drug has stopped. Heavy users are also more likely to suffer from brief episodes of 'amphetamine psychosis'; they may feel violent or aggressive, or experience paranoia or delusions, and they may hallucinate.

A common hallucination is the sensation that insects are crawling all over your body. Some people have made themselves bleed by scratching at their skin because of these non-existent bugs. This behaviour has also been seen in experiments where animals have been given amphetamines.

Although amphetamine psychosis usually wears off along with the drug, it can last for longer, and has been thought to trigger long-term psychiatric problems in some people.

Links with violence and aggressive behaviour

Violence, aggression and anti-social behaviour are common with heavy amphetamine use. In fact, people working in the field of drug abuse say that there are more amphetamine-related deaths due to violent behaviour than there are due to overdose. Many cases of domestic violence, suicide and murder have been linked with amphetamine use. This type of behaviour may be due to severe impairment of decision-making ability and general reasoning after taking amphetamines.

'Everybody used to say what a lovely boy Danny was. But since he started taking amphetamines, he's changed a lot. He's aggressive to his mum and me, and he can be violent – he got thrown out of a club last week for fighting.'
(Paul, Danny's father)

Armed forces

There are suggestions that use of the drugs by the armed forces has led to a number of incidents of 'friendly fire' (when soldiers bomb allied troops) and 'collateral damage' (when they bomb civilians).

Effects on the female body

Girls and women who use amphetamines may find that their periods are affected. There is little information available on how amphetamines affect the hormonal system, but we do know that female amphetamine users often find that their periods may be heavier or lighter, become irregular or even stop altogether. Also, because amphetamines dull the appetite, increase activity and often cause difficulty sleeping, they can affect the person's general health, and this could affect their periods too.

Women who use amphetamines while they are pregnant are at increased risk of miscarriage and premature labour. Babies born to amphetamine-using mothers tend to be smaller and develop more slowly. Some may have birth defects. Babies who are premature (born too soon) may suffer from a range of health problems. Those whose mothers used amphetamines late in their pregnancy may be born experiencing the effects of the drug. These babies may be over-active and agitated. They may cry constantly

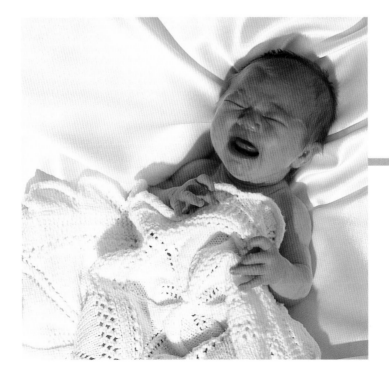

Sad start to life
Drugs taken by a woman while she is pregnant pass from her blood-stream into the baby's, and the baby will suffer side effects and withdrawal symptoms.

and be difficult to settle. Babies born to regular users may suffer withdrawal symptoms for the first few weeks of life. There is little research available about the effects of amphetamines on breastfeeding, but there is evidence to suggest that babies breastfed by mothers who are taking amphetamines tend to be poorly and irritable.

Women who use amphetamines and take the contraceptive pill are at increased risk, as both drugs can cause high blood pressure.

The dangers of injecting amphetamines

Some heavy amphetamine users inject the drug, because they find that this heightens its effects, giving a more intense 'rush'. People who inject drugs are known as IDUs (injecting drug users). Injecting amphetamines is particularly dangerous as it tends to lead to greater dependence and carries various health risks.

'I didn't even know you could inject speed until this girl at school told me about her brother. He's been really ill because he got an infected ulcer on his leg from injecting. That is so gross.'
(Hayley, aged 14)

Amphetamines are often 'cut' or mixed with other substances, any of which could cause blockages in the blood vessels. This may lead to organ damage. There is also the risk of collapsed veins, abscesses, and infections such as hepatitis and HIV. When someone injects, traces of their blood remain on the needle; if that person is infected, someone else using the same needle will inject infected blood straight into their own bloodstream.

Collapsed veins

Repeated injecting can result in collapsed veins. These eventually prevent the blood from circulating properly. The area where the blood cannot circulate may become swollen, turn blueish and be cold to the touch. If blood flow is severely restricted, areas of skin may die, and the affected part of the body may have to be amputated (removed by a surgeon during an operation). This death of skin tissue is called dry gangrene.

I thought it was safe

'I was really pleased with myself when I came off heroin after two years – I was getting scared that it might kill me. I was clean for a while, but then I started doing a bit of speed, just to liven myself up a bit, you know? Anyway, someone told me you could get a really good rush from injecting it. That was what I missed about heroin, so I thought, well, it's only a bit of speed, isn't it? It's not like it's addictive or anything.

But you start shooting up that stuff and you're as hooked as any heroin junkie. It's like you just can't stop doing it. Sometimes I'd be shooting up every couple of hours, just to keep the roll. Then of course you run out of needles, and you're not thinking straight so you start sharing.

Then I found out that I was positive – HIV. I don't know how I could have been so stupid – it was the main reason I stopped using heroin, then I go and pick it up off some speed freak. I'm not ill yet, but I could get ill any time. Injecting is so, so stupid – it's just a short cut to the cemetery.'
(Jay, aged 19)

Abscesses and ulcers

Reduced blood flow can also stop the body from healing properly, and so injection sites may become infected, causing boils or abscesses (inflamed, pus-filled swellings). Small scratches or knocks that do not heal properly may become ulcerated. Ulcers are extremely painful open sores, which can take months or years to heal.

Tetanus

Tetanus is an infection caused by bacteria that live in the soil and in the intestines of humans and other animals. The infection can enter the body through any open wound. Symptoms include muscle stiffness, headache and fever. If not treated quickly, it can lead to painful muscle spasms, breathing difficulties and even death.

Hepatitis

Hepatitis is serious inflammation of the liver, which can eventually trigger liver failure and cancer. Hepatitis is transmitted through contact with the bodily fluids of an infected person, so people who inject drugs and share needles are at risk.

HIV and AIDS

HIV (Human Immunodeficiency Virus) is carried in bodily fluids and can be transmitted through shared needles and through sexual intercourse with an infected person. HIV can lead to AIDS (Acquired Immunodeficiency Syndrome). When someone develops certain diseases and cancers as a result of HIV infection, they are diagnosed as having AIDS. Some of these conditions can be treated, but at present there is no cure and no vaccine.

Risk of overdose

The purity and strength of street amphetamines vary greatly, as the drugs are often mixed or 'cut' with other substances such as talcum powder, sugar or other stimulants such as caffeine. Therefore, users really cannot be sure exactly how much amphetamine they are putting into their bodies. This, together with the regular user's need for larger and larger doses in order to get the same effect, means that the risk of overdose is high.

Signs of amphetamine overdose

Common signs of amphetamine overdose include rapid or irregular heartbeat and raised blood pressure. Overdose can also cause chills or fever and sweating, seizures, difficulty breathing or hyperventilation, nausea and/or vomiting, nervousness, irritability, aggressive behaviour, overheating, dehydration and coma.

Overdose is more likely to occur as a result of injection, as IDUs are likely to inject higher doses than other people might use. Overdose can result in heart attacks or strokes, which may be fatal. The number of deaths due to amphetamine overdose is currently lower than that of deaths due to other drugs, such as heroin, but the figure does seem to be increasing.

Amphetamine users often use other drugs, such as sleeping pills or alcohol, in an attempt to relieve the insomnia caused by amphetamines. They may then take more amphetamines to relieve the drowsiness caused by the other drugs. This draws the user into a dangerous cycle of 'uppers' and 'downers'. It also increases the risk of accidental overdose.

'Every Saturday, some people think it's clever to snort rubbish up their noses or chuck it down their throats, often with booze. We save their lives, while some poor kid smashed up in a genuine accident has to wait in the next cubicle.'
(James, Accident and Emergency nurse)

Emergency
A drug overdose can be fatal, so the person needs urgent emergency treatment.

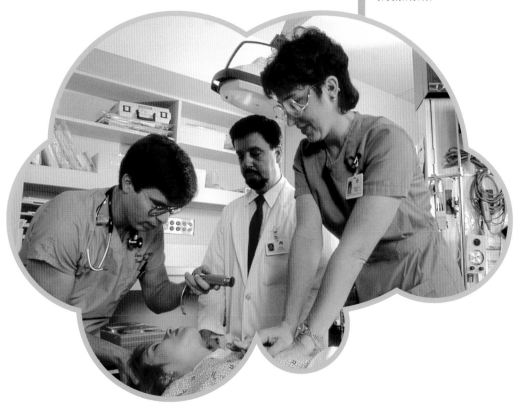

6 Addiction and dependence
The habit

Dopamine high
The first effect of amphetamine is to make the nerves in the brain produce more dopamine, and so the person feels 'high'.

How addiction works

Many people argue that amphetamines are not addictive. Addiction is defined by the medical profession as 'the repeated compulsive use of a substance, despite unpleasant or even life-threatening consequences'. This means that the person feels that something is driving them to use the drug again, and that they cannot resist it, even though they know that the results will be bad. In the case of amphetamines, it could be argued that use is not necessarily compulsive. However, most people working with problem drug users would agree that amphetamine users may reach a stage where they cannot manage without the drug. Some people suggest that, while many forms of amphetamine are not addictive, others, such as methamphetamine, are.

Some people working in the field of drug treatment argue that while one person may use a drug addictively – that is, repeatedly and compulsively, despite unpleasant consequences – another person may use the same drug in a non-addictive way, and will therefore not be seen as being addicted.

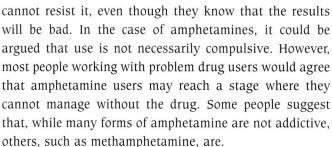

It is true that people seem to become addicted to some drugs more than to others. Heroin, for example, is said to be powerfully addictive. However, it could also be suggested that heroin attracts people who will behave addictively with any drug. Most heroin users are, in fact, 'polydrug users' – this means that they regularly use more than one drug. This is where the idea of the 'addictive personality' comes from: in other words, that some people become addicted to certain substances or types of behaviour more easily than other people.

Experts continue to argue about this. While they still don't know as much as they would like about the nature of addiction – there is little research on the subject – many believe that drug addiction usually involves both psychological and physical dependence.

'When I started using speed, everyone said it wasn't addictive, and that it couldn't do any harm. Well, I don't understand the medical stuff, but I do know I need it so often now that I've sold nearly everything to pay for it.' (Alex, aged 20)

Psychological dependence

When we do things we really enjoy, such as play our favourite sport, laugh at something, or go dancing – the natural 'highs' of daily life – our brains produce a chemical called dopamine, which creates vivid, positive memories of the experience. Amphetamines also trigger the production of dopamine, which acts as a sort of messenger, telling another part of the brain, 'the reward centre', that we feel great.

When someone takes amphetamines, much more dopamine is released than would occur normally. The user's brain feels intense pleasure during the amphetamine rush, and soon begins to associate taking amphetamines with feeling great. Taking amphetamines quickly becomes an experience that the user is keen to repeat.

Physical dependence

When people start using amphetamines, they usually need only a small dose in order to feel the effects. However, if they begin to use amphetamines regularly, their body quickly gets used to functioning with the drug present, and so ever-larger doses are needed to get the same effect. This is called 'tolerance'. Tolerance can build up to such a degree that even dangerously high doses of amphetamine produce little effect. Tolerance will fade if the person stops using the drug, but all too often, as tolerance builds and they take ever-larger amounts, they become so used to functioning with the drug that they become unable to function without it. In other words, they become dependent on the drug's effects just to get through a normal day.

Very soon, they no longer experience the pleasure that they associate with amphetamines. They find that they are taking the drug in order to relieve the unpleasant 'withdrawal symptoms' that they experience if they do not take it. When people have to take a drug in order to face the day or even just to function, they are said to have a 'drug dependence'.

Rats

Experiments with methamphetamine have shown that rats will self-administer the drug until they die.

Drug dependency

A person can become dependent on a prescription drug. This dependence is not the same as addiction.

What's the difference?

The difference between addiction and dependence is extremely difficult to pinpoint. Even people working in the field don't really understand why some people are defined as addicted and others as dependent. What is clear is that people can be dependent on a range of drugs without being addicted. For example, someone may be physically dependent on a drug to help them sleep, or to relieve pain. But they will not continue to use that drug compulsively despite unpleasant consequences. In fact, doctors note that many patients who have become dependent will voluntarily reduce their doses in an attempt to wean themselves off the drug. This is not how an addict would behave.

Some people argue that it is also possible to be addicted to something (for example, gambling, sex or exercise), without being physically dependent on it. The person's behaviour is continued and compulsive, and often has deeply unpleasant consequences, yet they are unable to stop.

How do you know if it's becoming a habit?

Many people start off using drugs as an occasional thing, perhaps when they go to parties or just at weekends. Yet even people who use amphetamines in this way can soon find that their use is out of control. If you are worried about amphetamine use, for yourself or someone else, or if you think that you or they may be developing dependency, think about how you or they might answer the following:

- Do you think about taking amphetamines more and more?

- Do you find it difficult to say 'no' if you are offered amphetamines?

- Do you find yourself needing to take the drug more often, and in larger doses, to get the same effect?

Addicted
Some people may be addicted to gambling, but they cannot be said to be dependent on it.

- Do you spend more money on amphetamines than you can afford?
- Do you keep saying you will stop using amphetamines but never do?
- Is your schoolwork, job, social life or relationship with your family affected by your amphetamine use?
- Are you tempted to take amphetamines on a weekday?
- Are you tempted to take amphetamines even when you are alone?

Anyone who answers 'yes' to any of these questions is showing signs of becoming dependent and should certainly think about getting some help to cut down or stop. The first step is to talk to someone about the problem. This may be a parent or family member, a teacher, school nurse or counsellor or perhaps a local priest. In some cases, people in the early stages of dependence may be able to wean themselves off the drug with the help and support of the people close to them.

A problem shared

Most people find that talking to someone about a worry or problem helps them to see things in perspective and find a way forward.

Withdrawal

Withdrawal symptoms occur when the body has become accustomed to receiving amphetamines and the supply stops. As we have seen, amphetamines cause the user to feel more alert, confident and energetic. The person feels on a 'high', and, if they 'top up' the doses of amphetamines, the high may last for several days. But the higher the high, the lower the low that follows. The body's natural stores of energy will have become depleted, and the user is likely to experience a 'crash' – sudden, severe withdrawal symptoms, such as extreme tiredness, fatigue and depression.

It is easy to understand how the amphetamine user, when faced with these unpleasant symptoms, feels tempted to take another dose to avoid or relieve them. It is the cycle of highs and lows that draws the user into heavier and more frequent use.

Withdrawal symptoms

If someone who has become dependent on amphetamines stops taking them, they will have withdrawal symptoms as their body gets used to functioning without the drug. These may include:

- intense hunger;
- extreme tiredness – sometimes a need to sleep for up to three days;
- fatigue, loss of energy;
- irritability;
- restless sleep, nightmares;
- depression, which may be severe;
- nausea;
- palpitations;
- hyperventilation;
- fearfulness and anxiety;
- powerful craving for amphetamines.

Binge use

Some amphetamine users take their drugs regularly. Others may use them only occasionally – when they go to a dance event, perhaps, or when they feel they need the stimulant effects of the drug to stay awake for a long period. Many users fall into a pattern of binge use – every now and then consuming several large doses over a fairly short period, such as two, three or four days. Using amphetamines like this is sometimes called a 'speed run'.

Heavy users may inject themselves every few hours, only stopping when they have run out of the drug or reached a point of physical exhaustion, delirium – a state of mental

A dream job

Justin, aged 19, began training to be a chef when he was 17. His dreams came true when he was offered a trainee position in a top restaurant.

'I was over the moon,' says Justin. 'I loved it – the atmosphere, the pressure, the banter among the chefs. I made loads of friends and we all helped each other out. The kitchen was really busy at weekends – totally manic. Some of the guys used speed to help them get through, and when I was offered some, I thought, why not? It was great. I got loads done. I finished all the prep, got everything ready on time during service, and cleaned down the head chef's work area. He was well pleased. Soon I was using it every weekend, and I kept topping up so I could go out after my shift. I'd be speeding for ages, then I'd come down and just sleep for days. I kept missing shifts because I was still asleep or, even if I did wake up, I was so wiped out I couldn't work. In the end, they fired me. I've got another kitchen job now, but it's only a canteen. I'll never use that stuff again. It may have ruined my career for good.'

confusion and disorientation – or psychosis. During this period of heavy use, the user becomes focused on recreating the initial euphoric rush, losing interest in anything else, including food. When someone uses amphetamines in this way, tolerance can develop very quickly, and the level of dependence is quite high. When the person stops using the drug after a binge, they will often experience depression, anxiety, craving and extreme fatigue. Essentially, their 'high' is followed by a 'crash'.

Using more than one drug

People who use more than one drug at a time are called 'polydrug users'. Polydrug use is fairly common among amphetamine users as people often take other drugs in order to counteract the unpleasant side effects of amphetamines. They may take cannabis or opiates to calm them down or to help them sleep, or they may try anti-depressants to help relieve the 'low' feeling they get after coming down from an amphetamine high.

Taking a cocktail of drugs like this can be extremely dangerous, as there is no way of knowing how the body will react. In some cases, the risk of death is greatly increased. It is particularly dangerous to use amphetamines with other stimulants, such as ecstasy. As both these drugs raise the heart rate and blood pressure, the risk of death through stroke or heart attack is increased. Taking amphetamines with alcohol can increase the risk of aggressive or violent behaviour, and can also cause liver or kidney failure, both of which can be fatal. Depending on what the person takes, they also risk becoming addicted to or dependent on the other substance, as well as amphetamines.

Drugs killed our daughter

'It would have been Hannah's eighteenth birthday next Friday. We'd planned a surprise party at an Italian restaurant in town. She loved going out to restaurants – said it gave her a chance to dress up. We were going to take her out beforehand to buy a new outfit – she loved clothes, and she could wear anything. She was so beautiful. I still can't get my head around the fact that she'd been taking drugs. Her friends said she'd taken these drugs before. Apparently, she'd tried ecstasy a couple of times, and she'd also dabbled with speed. But this time, she took them both together. They said it was because they were going to a dance club and they wanted to be able to keep going all night. The coroner said she'd died of a massive stroke – a blood vessel burst in her brain. The funeral was awful. When they put her coffin into the ground, I started screaming. I passed out in the end. You never think you're going to bury your own child.'
(Diane, Hannah's mum)

7 The outlook for amphetamine users
Can the damage be repaired?

A safe drug?

Many people argue that, as death from overdose is not common, amphetamine is a relatively 'safe' drug. But, as we have seen, short-term use can cause unpleasant side effects and social problems, with some people losing their jobs due to the effects of the drug. Long-term use can have more serious consequences, including psychiatric problems such as severe depression and psychosis.

If someone becomes dependent on a drug, it can be very difficult for them to stop using it, even if they are not 'addicted' in the medical sense. If their use continues, the unpleasant side effects will obviously continue and may get worse. Therefore it is important for dependent users to recognize that their amphetamine use is damaging their lives. They need to get help to reduce their use, reduce the risks to their health and, hopefully, to eventually stop using the drug altogether.

'I kept falling asleep at school, especially on Mondays when I'd been speeding all weekend. They kept asking me why, and in the end I admitted it. I've been seeing the school counsellors about it, and I'm trying really hard to stop.' (Jason, aged 16)

How do you know if someone is using amphetamines?

One of the first signs that someone is using drugs is that they start to behave differently. This may include hanging out with a different group of people, taking less interest in their appearance, in their family or in school or work. People who are using amphetamines or other stimulants are often restless and jumpy or fidgety. They may talk very quickly, be irritable or aggressive, or may seem nervous and anxious. They also tend to have a poor appetite, which soon leads to weight loss, and they will often be unable to sleep. Periods of sleeplessness are often followed by long periods of unusual fatigue and tiredness, perhaps causing the person to sleep for long periods, including during the day.

Looking out

Friends look out for each other, and are good at noticing if someone is behaving differently from normal, or if something may be wrong.

Change of character

'I started using speed to get through my exams, but I really loved the buzz, and I got into doing it at weekends for clubbing and parties and stuff. Most of my friends stuck to weekends, but I got used to feeling wide awake and full of energy, and I started doing it more and more often. In the end, it was almost every day. The only days I didn't use it was when I was sleeping it off. But I didn't realize how it was changing my personality. I'd started to get irritable and moody, snapping at everyone, accusing them of talking about me behind my back. One day, my little sister, Holly – she's only seven – was dancing around, like kids do, singing some song and giggling. I shouted at her for making too much noise, but she just carried on, so I hit her, slapped her on the face, so hard that it left a mark. I'll never forget how she cried. My boyfriend, Adam, said he'd had enough. He said either I stopped using speed altogether, or it was over between us. He persuaded me to tell my parents and, with their help and his, I stopped using it. It was hard for the first few weeks – like breaking any habit. And I felt quite down and wiped out, but I got over it. And I think Holly's forgiven me.'
(Lucy, aged 18)

Self-help

Sometimes it is largely a question of looking at why the person started using drugs in the first place, and why that use has gone out of control. For example, if someone started using amphetamines to stay awake all night for a party, and then continued because they liked the 'full-of-energy' feeling associated with the drug, then maybe they could look at other ways of boosting their energy, perhaps by changing their diet or simply getting more sleep.

If someone's amphetamine use is linked with other problem areas of their life, such as depression or problems with relationships or housing, or if their amphetamine use is particularly heavy or dangerous, as in the case of someone who is injecting the drug, they should seek professional help. The family doctor will be able to advise on the possible courses of action, or the user could contact a local drug advice service, who will be aware of what help is available in the area.

'I'd been depressed for ages, but hadn't really admitted it. I used speed to blot things out. I saw my doctor eventually, and he put me on a course of anti-depressants. I'm coping much better now, and my doctor's been great.'
(Paul, aged 19)

Treatment

Treatment for amphetamine dependence is not as well developed as treatment for addiction to some other drugs, such as heroin. This may be because there is considerable debate as to whether amphetamines are truly addictive. However, it is widely suggested that stronger forms of the drug, such as methamphetamine, are highly addictive, especially when injected, and many professionals working in the field are keen to improve support and treatment services for people who are affected. There is very little evidence of the effectiveness or otherwise of the treatments that are currently available.

One controversial form of treatment is to prescribe low doses of amphetamines for problem users. This means that, although their amphetamine use is continuing, the amount and purity of what they use is controlled, making overdose much less likely, and hopefully reducing their dependence. Some people argue that prescribing amphetamines is unethical, because of the risk of the person developing psychosis due to long-term use. However, the results from on-going studies are encouraging, and show that this approach attracts many users into treatment and reduces their level of injecting and needle sharing.

No-one knows about amphetamine addicts

'I've worked with speed addicts for years. It makes me really angry when people say it's not addictive – as if that means it's not dangerous! They should see some of the poor devils I've had to deal with. Even if it's not addictive in the same way that heroin is, it can still do serious damage to someone's life. But no-one seems to be doing anything about the problem. Heroin addicts are prescribed substitutes to help them come off it, but the idea that we could do that for speed addicts is frowned upon. Injecting is becoming more and more common, and you're even getting ex-heroin users moving to speed because it's so much easier to get hold of. Trouble is, if they start shooting up, they're as likely to die of AIDS or something as they were when they were still using smack. There are plenty of needle exchanges around, but they seem to only target heroin users. Everyone's heard of heroin, everyone knows it can kill you. But ask people about amphetamines, and they'll tell you it was a '60s drug, and they've often never even heard of people injecting it. We've got to get the message out there that amphetamine use is still widespread, and it's still causing untold misery.'
(Mark, drug project worker)

Some experts suggest that the prescription for amphetamines can be seen as 'the carrot that entices amphetamine users through the door of the treatment centre'. They argue that, if the chance of being given the drug makes people come forward, then this is a major step in reaching a group of problem drug users who, at the moment, see no point in attending drug treatment agencies because so little help is available. As amphetamine users are the second largest group of people who regularly inject drugs (after heroin users), it is important that the practice of needle sharing is addressed and, if possible, reduced.

Another way of treating amphetamine dependency is to prescribe anti-depressants, often combined with counselling. This may help to address the issues that led the person to become a problem drug user in the first place. One of the reasons people become addicted or

Needle exchange schemes

Needle exchange schemes can reduce the risk of harm to injecting drug users (IDUs). In the UK, most schemes are publicly funded, while in the USA, this varies from state to state. The schemes work by offering users sterile syringes and needles, which they return for disposal after use, in exchange for new ones. This reduces the risk of spreading HIV, hepatitis and other blood-borne infections. The needle exchange schemes may also offer advice and counselling on drug problems and other health, social and welfare issues.

The schemes are a good way of getting information to drug users about the treatment and services that are available. Currently, the main users of the schemes are heroin addicts, largely because they are the largest group of IDUs, but also because many injecting amphetamine users are unaware that such schemes can help them. Some people argue that providing clean needles in this way increases intravenous drug use, but there is no evidence to support this. Research from several countries suggests that the schemes are effective and can significantly reduce risky behaviour.

dependent is that amphetamines increase the levels of brain chemicals responsible for mood and feelings of wellbeing. When the person comes down from the amphetamine high, the levels of those chemicals fall dramatically, causing the user to feel low or depressed. Anti-depressants can help balance the brain chemistry, removing what the user sees as the 'need' for more amphetamines.

Education and discussion

Amphetamines do seem to be a little-known drug, but their use still does considerable damage to people's health, wealth, career plans and relationships. Perhaps one of the best approaches to dealing with the problem is to focus on education, so that more people understand the facts about the drug, in particular its potential for harm. It is especially important for young people to know about amphetamines, as they are the most likely to come into contact with the drug. By arming ourselves with knowledge about amphetamine use and its dangers, and through open and honest discussion, perhaps we can help to inform and protect our friends, colleagues and even future generations from this destructive yet all too common drug.

Developing views

It can be helpful to share ideas and opinions about drugs, bringing the subject into the open.

Glossary

addiction   when someone needs a drug in order to relieve unpleasant symptoms experienced when they stop taking it. This happens because the body has adapted to the drug being present, so when it is not present, the body craves it.

adrenaline   a hormone produced by the body in response to fear, such as when threatened with attack.

attention deficit hyperactivity disorder (ADHD)   a disorder affecting children and young people, characterized by difficult behaviour and poor attention span.

base   amphetamine in the form of a putty-like substance.

caffeine   a chemical that occurs naturally in coffee, tea and cocoa and acts as a mild stimulant.

central nervous system   the brain and spinal cord, where 'messages' move from the brain to various parts of the body.

coma   deep unconsciousness caused by injury, illness or poison.

compound   a combination of two or more chemical substances.

compulsive   describes an action that somebody is compelled to take – they cannot resist it or control it, as in the sort of behaviour that occurs with addiction.

controversial   causing disagreement and argument, as in the practice of prescribing amphetamines.

delusion   believing something to be true when it is not, a false belief.

dependence   powerful physical and/or psychological craving for a substance. Physical dependence occurs when the body becomes used to functioning with the drug present. Psychological dependence occurs when the person feels that they cannot go about their normal life without taking the drug.

dopamine   a brain chemical that regulates emotion.

euphoria   a feeling of extreme pleasure and happiness.

hallucination   when someone sees, hears, smells or feels something that isn't really there.

hepatitis   inflammation of the liver.

immune system   the body's natural defence system, responsible for protection against and fighting of infection.

intravenous   into the vein (as in an injection).

lethargy   extreme tiredness or weariness.

methamphet-amine   a particularly strong form of amphetamine.

narcolepsy   a condition that causes the sufferer to frequently fall deeply asleep, even at inappropriate times, such as in the middle of a meal, or while talking to someone.

nausea	feeling sick.
neurone	a nerve cell that transmits chemical signals/messages.
noradrenaline	a body chemical that increases blood pressure and breathing rate.
obesity	extreme overweight.
paranoia	the feeling that everyone is against you. When someone has paranoia, they may think that others want to hurt them, are criticizing them or are 'out to get' them.
polydrug user	someone who uses more than one drug.
psychosis	when someone loses touch with reality. They may suffer delusions, paranoia and hallucinations.
recreational	purely for fun or entertainment.
Ritalin	amphetamine-based drug that is used to treat ADHD.
rush	term used to describe sudden feeling of euphoria experienced by some amphetamine users.
serotonin	a brain chemical involved in various brain functions to do with mood and emotion.
snorting	inhaling a powdered drug sharply through the nose, often through a rolled-up bank note.
soluble	easily dissolved.
'speeding'	slang term describing someone who is under the influence of amphetamines.
stimulant	something that activates the mind or body, making it work faster and harder than usual.
stroke	illness caused by an interruption to the brain's blood supply, for example when a blood vessel in the brain bursts or becomes blocked. There may be temporary or permanent paralysis, or loss of consciousness.
sympathetic nervous system	a division of the central nervous system that controls many involuntary actions of the organs, glands and other parts of the body.
synthesize	to create artificially.
tolerance	when the body adjusts to the presence of a substance, meaning that more is needed to create a reaction.
withdrawal	the process of coming off an addictive substance.

Resources

National Drugs Helpline

Tel: 0800 776600

Confidential advice.

Drugscope

Tel: 020 7928 1211

www.drugscope.org.uk

Advice and information on all aspects of drug use.

ADFAM National

Tel: 020 7928 8900

Support and information helpline for families and friends of drug users.

Release

Tel: 020 7729 5255

www.release.org.uk

Confidential advice on drug use and related legal issues.

ChildLine

Telephone: 0800 1111

National 24-hour helpline for children and young people in danger, distress or with any type of problem.

National AIDS helpline

Telephone: 0800 012 322

Advice and information about HIV and AIDS related issues.

Child Bereavement Trust

Aston House, The High Street, West Wycombe, High Wycombe, Bucks HP14 3AG

www.childbereavementtrust.org.uk

Advice and resources for children and young people coping with bereavement.

Further Reading

Amphetamines – Danger in the Fast Lane, by Scott E. Lukas (Chelsea House, 1992)

Looks at the history, effects and medical and legal aspects of amphetamine use and abuse.

Need to Know: Amphetamines, by Rob Alcraft (Heinemann, 2001)

Non-judgemental, non-patronizing information book for teenagers.

Buzzed: The Straight Dope about the Most Used and Abused Drugs from Alcohol to Ecstasy, by Cynthia Kuhn et al (Norton, 1998)

An in-depth look at drugs, how they work and what they can do to you.

Different Like Me: A Book for Teenagers Who Worry about Their Parent's Use of Alcohol/Drugs, by Evelyn Leite and Pamela Espelan (Johnson Institute, 1989)

Offers practical advice and suggestions for teens battling with a parent's addiction.

Disclaimer

The website addresses (URLs) included in this book were valid at the time of going to press. However, because of the nature of the internet, it is possible that some addresses may have changed, or sites may have changed or closed down since publication. While the author and the publishers regret any inconvenience this may cause readers, no responsibility for any such changes can be accepted by either the author or the publishers.

Index